HALLE BERRY

"Beauty Is Not Just Physical"

Michael A. Schuman

Series Consultant:
Dr. Russell L. Adams, Chairman
Department of
Afro-American Studies,
Howard University

Enslow Publishers, Inc.

40 Industrial Road   PO Box 38
Box 398   Aldershot
Berkeley Heights, NJ 07922   Hants GU12 6BP
USA   UK

http://www.enslow.com

"BEAUTY IS NOT JUST PHYSICAL.
IT'S ABOUT WHAT YOU STAND FOR,
HOW YOU LIVE YOUR LIFE."
—*Halle Berry*

Author's Dedication
To my friend Paul Teitelman, also a fine actor—and director.

Library of Congress Cataloging-in-Publication Data

Schuman, Michael.
    Halle Berry : "beauty is not just physical" / Michael A. Schuman.
        p. cm. — (African-American biography library)
    Filmography: p.
    Includes bibliographical references and index.
    ISBN-10: 0-7660-2467-9
    1. Berry, Halle—Juvenile literature. 2. Motion picture actors and actresses—United
States—Biography—Juvenile literature. 3. African American motion picture actors and
actresses—Biography—Juvenile literature. I. Title. II. Series.
    PN2287.B4377S38 2006
    791.4302'8'092—dc22
                                            2005017155
    ISBN-13: 978-0-7660-2467-0

Printed in the United States of America

10 9 8 7 6 5 4 3

To Our Readers:
We have done our best to make sure all Internet Addresses in this book were active and appropriate when we went to press. However, the author and the publisher have no control over and assume no liability for the material available on those Internet sites or on other Web sites they may link to. Any comments or suggestions can be sent by e-mail to comments@enslow.com or to the address on the back cover.

Every effort has been made to locate all copyright holders of material used in this book. If any errors or omissions have occurred, corrections will be made in future editions of this book.

Illustration Credits: AP/Wide World, pp. 4, 8 (all), 21, 24, 29, 43, 49, 64, 67, 73, 81, 82, 86, 88, 91, 93, 94; Classmates.com, pp. 15, 16, 18; Everett Collection, pp. 32, 34, 38, 46, 51, 58, 61, 70, 75, 78, 90, 97.

Cover Photographs: AP/Wide World (portrait); © Corel Corporation (Hollywood sign).

Contents

Berry brought her mother to the Academy Awards.

◆◆◆◆◆

Chapter 1

"And the Oscar Goes to . . ."

The air buzzed with anticipation and excitement as Hollywood's finest actors, directors, and more arrived at the Kodak Theater in Hollywood, California, on March 24, 2002. It was the night of the Academy Awards ceremony, the most talked-about event of the year for the motion picture industry. The women's gowns had been crafted by the world's top designers, and the men looked dapper in their expensive suits. Hundreds of fans waved and cheered as the cream of Hollywood entered the theater.

Among the performers in attendance that night was thirty-five-year-old Halle Berry, who began her career not as an actress but as a model. In fact, some people—both movie critics and moviegoers alike—believed at first that her beauty was the main reason for her success. Berry has said, "Frankly, fighting against my looks has become a large part of my career as an actress. I mean, everyone should have such problems, but producers never consider me for anything that isn't glamorous."[1]

Berry had received her first Oscar nomination that year, for best actress in a lead role. Of the hundreds of performers who appear in movies every year, only five men and five women can be named in each category. While being nominated is an honor, winning an Oscar is the ultimate achievement. Winners are selected by tallying the votes of academy members.

Berry had been nominated for her starring role in the movie *Monster's Ball*. It is a dark drama about the African-American widow of an executed convicted murderer. She falls in love with a prison guard, later learning that he had been directly involved in executing her husband. "Monster's ball" is an old English term for a condemned man's last meal.

In *Monster's Ball*, Berry plays a poor, dowdy waitress. She appears to be wearing no makeup and spends much of the movie in a

The Oscars

The Academy of Motion Picture Arts and Sciences Awards ceremony takes place annually in February or March, when the movie industry honors the best work in motion pictures for the previous year. The presentation of the awards, also called Oscars, is televised live in dozens of countries across the world. Categories include all aspects of the movie industry, with technical awards for lighting and sound technicians as well as artistic awards for the best actors.

waitress's uniform. One reason she had wanted the part was that it provided a challenge. At first, the producer Lee Daniels told her, "Listen, you're simply not right for this. You're too beautiful for the role."[2]

Berry refused to take no for an answer. She asked Daniels if he was saying that all poor and troubled people are ugly. She asked him why African Americans had to be stereotyped into certain categories. Daniels, who is also African American, realized that she had a point. Berry wanted so much to be in this movie that she took a pay cut to do so. She had been paid $2.5 million for her previous movie, *Swordfish*, but accepted $600,000—less than a quarter of her payment for *Swordfish*—to take the role in *Monster's Ball*.[3]

> "Fighting against my looks has become a large part of my career as an actress."

The critics' reviews of her performance in *Monster's Ball* were mostly positive, but the odds of winning the Oscar were not in Berry's favor. For one thing, the film had been produced by a little independent studio called Lion's Gate. Huge studios such as Universal and MGM advertise in the major movie industry publications, urging academy members to vote for their movies. Lion's Gate could not afford such publicity. In addition, the director of *Monster's Ball*, Marc Forster, was almost unknown in the movie business, with only two other films to his credit.

Until 2002, the trailblazing actors Hattie McDaniel (1939), left;
Sidney Poitier (1964), center; and Whoopi Goldberg (1990), right,
were the only African-American Academy Award winners.

Finally, there was the race factor. While Berry is of mixed heritage, most people view her as African American. In the seventy-three years of Academy Awards, no African American had ever been named best lead actress. Two African-American women had won for best supporting actress: Hattie McDaniel, for her role in the 1939 classic *Gone With the Wind*; and Whoopi Goldberg, for the 1990 movie *Ghost*. At that time, Sidney Poitier, named best lead actor for the 1964 movie *Lilies of the Field*, was the only African American to have won the top honor.

Berry nervously awaited the name of the winner in her category. It would be announced near the end of the ceremony. Berry's fellow nominees were all stellar actresses: Sissy Spacek, Renée Zellweger, Nicole Kidman, and Dame Judi Dench. Berry later recalled, "I remember sitting in the auditorium and watching clips of Sissy and Renée and Nicole and thinking, 'Halle, you're nuts to think you could ever win.'"[4]

Finally, after nearly three hours of presentations, the time came to announce the best actress. Actor Russell Crowe read the list of nominees. "And the Oscar goes to"—Crowe paused dramatically as he opened the envelope—"Halle Berry." The camera turned to Berry, who was crying. She looked stunned as she made her way to the stage. Crowe saw how flustered she was and whispered in her ear, "Breathe, mate. Just breathe. It's going to be okay."[5]

Berry tried to compose herself, but raw emotions took over. She gave a rambling, tear-filled speech.

> Oh, my God. Oh, my God. I'm sorry. This moment is so much bigger than me. This moment is for Dorothy Dandridge, Lena Horne, Diahann Carroll. It's for the women that stand beside me, Jada Pinkett, Angela Bassett, Viveca Fox. And it's for every nameless, faceless woman of color that now has a chance because this door tonight has been opened. Thank you. I'm so honored. I'm so honored. And I thank the Academy for choosing me to be the vessel for which His blessing might flow.[6]

Halle Berry had made history.

Chapter 2

"Beautiful in My Own Right"

Halle Maria Berry was born on August 14, 1966, in Cleveland City Hospital in Cleveland, Ohio. Halle's father, Jerome Berry, was an orderly who worked in the Veterans Administration Hospital in Cleveland. There he met Judith Hawkins, a psychiatric nurse. Hawkins had been born in Liverpool, England. Her family moved across the Atlantic Ocean to Ohio when she was six.

Berry, a black man, and Hawkins, a white woman, fell in love and married in the 1960s. At that time, interracial couples were not accepted by much of American society. In some states, interracial marriages were illegal. Although Jerome and Judith Berry were not breaking any laws in Ohio, they still faced difficulties as a mixed-race couple.

The Berrys' first daughter, Heidi, was born in 1964. Then Judith became pregnant with Halle. One day, she happened to be shopping at a downtown Cleveland department store called Halle Brothers. Looking at the store's shopping bags, she decided that she really liked the name Halle. So the new baby was named after a department store.

The Berry family settled in a mostly African-American neighborhood in Cleveland. Judith was a doting mother who dressed her girls in the best clothing she could afford.

For Halle, the early years were not happy ones. Many members of both Jerome's and Judith's families were against the interracial marriage. Some of them completely ignored the couple. Holidays and birthdays that should have been happy occasions were often spent without extended family. Halle's mixed-race family often received disapproving stares from strangers when in public.

The Berrys had an even bigger problem: Halle's father was an alcoholic who became physically abusive when drinking. When he was drunk, he would slap and punch his wife. If Heidi interfered and tried to stop her father, Jerome beat her, too.[1] Halle stayed out of the way. She later said, "He never hit me. He beat on my sister, but never me. I felt a lot of guilt. When my sister saw him hitting my mother, she would jump in and get hit, but I would run and hide."[2]

In a moment of rage one day during dinner, Halle's father picked up the family's pet dog and threw it across the dining room. The tiny dog hit the wall and nearly bit

> For Halle, the early years were not happy ones.

its tongue off. Halle later said, "I remember thinking, 'God, let him leave,' so my life could get back to normal."[3] She got her wish. Jerome Berry moved out of the house when Halle was four. The Berrys would go on as a family of three.

In elementary school, Halle was a quiet girl. Her sister, Heidi, was more outgoing. Halle was regarded by her teachers as a smart child who loved to read. But no matter what kind of student she was, Halle could not escape being treated differently because of her racial heritage. Some of Halle's African-American classmates called her a liar because they did not believe that a white woman could be her biological mother. Other children believed Halle, but picked on her just for having a white mother.

When Halle was in fourth grade, her family moved from Cleveland's inner city to a mainly white suburb called Oakwood Village. Judith thought her children would receive a better education there. Halle did well in her new school, but prejudice followed her.

Kids called the Berry sisters "zebras," for half black, half white. They also teased Halle and Heidi with another unwelcome nickname: "Oreo cookie," meaning black on the outside and white on the inside. For a while, Halle was getting Oreo cookies in the mail. At first she thought one of the boys had a crush on her. Finally, she realized that the cookies were not a gift but a racial insult.

The racial difference was just as tough on her mother. Berry said about her new neighborhood, "The culture shock was something you can't imagine. I remember the fury my mother would feel in line at the grocery store because the people around us looked puzzled; they assumed these black kids couldn't possibly be her children."[4]

Judith tried her best to give Halle a dose of reality. Although Halle knew she was equal parts white and African-American, Judith was aware of how her daughter would be treated when strangers saw her coffee-colored skin. Judith said, "When you leave this house, people will assume you're black. And you'll be discriminated against. So accept being black. Embrace it."[5]

In fifth grade, Halle met a role model who would instill pride and confidence in her. Yvonne Nichols Sims was Halle's fifth-grade teacher. Berry admired her as a caring and intelligent woman. To this day, the two keep in touch. Berry said, "My fifth-grade teacher was a black woman. She sort of took me in, thank God, because I could have been one of those kids who really had a crisis with [race]. She taught me that I was beautiful in my own right."[6]

Judith Berry was no less a role model than Yvonne Sims. When Halle was ten, her father returned and asked Judith to take him back. She did, and he spent a year living with his wife and daughters. Judith had hoped he had changed and learned to control his drinking. "She wanted us to have him in our lives," said Halle.[7]

In spite of Judith's dream of a happy family life, it was not to be. According to Halle, "It was the worst year of our lives. I'd been praying for my father, and when I got him I just wanted him to leave. My mother would cry; they would fight. It was scary. He was still an alcoholic."[8] After a year, Judith told Jerome to leave. Jerome Berry would never again have close contact with his wife or children.

Judith tried to reassure Halle that their home situation was not her fault. She repeatedly told her daughter that she was special, but Halle had trouble getting the message to sink in. Later, she said, "I always had a feeling of not being good enough that came from my father leaving."[9]

Because of her training as a psychiatric nurse, Judith knew about the benefits of mental health treatment for children in such an uneasy home situation. So at the age of ten, Halle began regular sessions with a psychiatrist. Halle said that her mother, "saw that my mental state—as well as my sister's—was at risk, and she made sure we had an appropriate outlet for discussing our feelings. What a gift! To learn at such an early age that there is a calm and effective way to process major emotions was a lesson I've never forgotten."[10]

Although therapy gave Berry an outlet for her emotions, it did not solve all her problems. Halle went out of her way to be the best at everything she did—not just in her classes, but in extracurricular activities, too. "It was sickening how much I craved being liked," said Halle later.[11]

In middle school, Halle became a class monitor and a cheerleader. Being a cheerleader helped Halle break out of her shyness. However, there were new problems that came with the territory. A lot of the other girls thought all cheerleaders were stuck up, and they accused Halle of thinking she was better than others. The girls who held grudges against Halle and envied her good looks could never have known that inside she still felt as if she was not good enough.

Halle in her eighth-grade junior high school yearbook in 1980.

In high school, Halle participated in more and more extracurricular activities. And she always had to be the best. "I was Miss Everything—cheerleader, student senator, on the newspaper, the honor roll, you name it," said Berry.[12]

Halle was elected freshman class president, and three years later she was voted president of the senior class. Halle was recommended for the National Honor Society. She also had a steady boyfriend, a popular football player named LaShawn Boyd. It seemed as if she was finally being accepted by her classmates. Then came the vote for queen of the senior prom.

Berry was elected prom queen by a wide margin. But some classmates accused her of stealing the title by stuffing the ballot box—that is, having her supporters vote for her

Cheerleading and other extracurricular activities
helped Halle overcome her shyness.

more than once. That was not possible, because the voting
had been monitored, but the accusation stuck. Some
students claimed that the runner-up, a white girl with
blond hair, was the true winner. Berry later said, "They
weren't about to have a black prom queen, so they accused
me of stuffing the ballot box. When it came to academics,
I was always an A student and they were comfortable
with that. But when it came to being the queen, that
was something different. And so they decided there
would be co-queens. Me and this White, blond, blue-eyed
all-American girl."[13] The words of Halle's mother—that
people would always see her as black—rang true.

When school officials still heard grumbling, they decided the only way to settle the matter was to have a coin toss. Halle chose "heads," and the coin came up heads. Halle would reign as prom queen.

The whole experience had been so unpleasant that Halle decided not to show up at the prom. Again it was Halle's mother who advised her. If Halle did not show up, Judith said, she would be giving her enemies a victory since they did not want her in the first place. So Halle did attend, but as a protest she arrived thirty minutes before the end of the evening. The first sight that greeted Halle when she arrived was the entire prom committee standing in the hall, wondering about their missing queen.

Ironically, the future actress did not take part in any of her school plays, something she blames on being a racial minority. "Juliet can't be black," she said, referring to the female lead in William Shakespeare's *Romeo and Juliet*. "It was very limited in what we could do."[14]

While her high school friend Terrie Fitzwater agrees that racial discrimination took place, not all of her classmates saw it that way. Another student, Kelli Hichens, said, "Halle Berry was a very well-liked girl in school. She had friends who were both black and white."[15]

Since she enjoyed working on her school newspaper, Halle decided to study broadcast journalism at nearby Cuyahoga Community College. She took courses there and also worked at a local radio station. However, she

For Halle, being elected prom queen turned out
to be a hard life lesson in discrimination.

felt uncomfortable asking personal questions during
interviews. Once, she had to talk to a family whose house
had just burned down. She was so upset by the tragedy
that she lost her composure and began crying during the
interview. She realized she did not have the emotional
toughness for that type of work.

Although Berry did not act in plays as a teenager, she did
take to the stage in another role. While Berry was attending
community college, a boyfriend secretly entered her in the
Miss Teen Ohio contest. A few weeks later, Berry received a
letter from the beauty pageant officials, telling her she
had been accepted as a contestant. What was going on?

It was then that her boyfriend confessed to submitting two photographs of Berry.

Beauty pageant contestants are often vying for college scholarships. The possibility of winning scholarship money made the idea of a beauty contest more inviting. Berry also still felt the need to prove to herself that she was an attractive and intelligent woman, and winning such a pageant could cement those feelings.

But again, race could be an issue. The nation's most famous beauty pageant, the Miss America pageant, did not have an African-American winner until Vanessa Williams won the crown in 1983. For many years, African Americans held their own, separate contests.

There are varying explanations for the racially divided pageants. Some say it was due to racism. Others believe it was because the standard of beauty in the United States leaned toward blond women with fair skin (although the majority of Miss America winners have been brunettes).[16] Carl Dunn, a pageant historian, believes it was because African Americans historically did not take part in open beauty contests. He said, "I don't think there was a racist agenda. I don't think anyone ever said, 'This lady is black so she's not going to win.' Nowadays, there are more African Americans entering so there are more African Americans winning."[17] Regardless, Berry wanted to prove

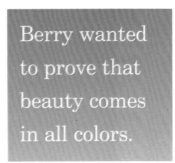

Berry wanted to prove that beauty comes in all colors.

that beauty comes in all colors. So after much consideration, she decided to take some time off from college to enter the Miss Teen Ohio pageant in 1984.

With her good looks and charm, Berry won the pageant for Miss Teen Ohio of 1985. She said, "It was crazy, a total fluke, but that experience gave me the confidence to go out there and try new things."[18] That victory qualified her to enter the national pageant, Miss Teen America, held later in 1984. Berry won that as well.

After her success in these endeavors, Berry decided to try her luck in more pageants. In 1986 she entered the Miss Ohio contest. The winner of this pageant would represent

Beauty Pageants

For decades, beauty pageants were very popular. There are many different ones, but the most famous is the Miss America pageant. As the feminist movement gathered steam in the late 1960s, many women began questioning the purpose of such contests. Even though pageants often include talent competitions, and although participants are questioned about their goals and ideals, contestants are traditionally judged mostly on their looks. Both women and men began to wonder whether that was a positive way to view a woman's worth. Today, the Miss America pageant and others continue to attract dedicated fans, but their popularity has declined.

First-runner-up Halle Berry lost the 1986
Miss USA pageant to Christy Fichtner, right.

her state in the national competition for Miss USA. Berry's winning streak held, and she was named Miss Ohio. Then, in the Miss USA pageant, Berry came in second.

Although Berry did not win the title crown, being first runner-up had its pluses. She was invited to go on a seven-nation tour with the legendary comedian Bob Hope, entertaining United States military personnel overseas. And while Miss USA, Christy Fichtner, went on to represent the United States in the Miss Universe contest, Berry was eligible to compete in the Miss World pageant in 1987. That meant another exotic trip, this time to London, where the pageant was held.

> "I spent a lot of time with a crown on my head."[19]

Berry finished the Miss World pageant in a respectable third place. In later years, she voiced mixed feelings about her experiences with beauty pageants. In 1995, she said, "Pageants teach you how to lose and not be devastated. It was great preparation for Hollywood."[20]

In 2002 she expressed regret over taking part in beauty contests "in many ways, because it perpetuated my physical self a lot more than I ever wanted to. But it was also very significant in a way, because I gained a lot of confidence in myself. That confidence has served me throughout my life. So I got something meaningful out of it. But most of what the pageant was about was superficial."[21]

One of the judges for Miss USA—a Chicago-based modeling agent named Kay Mitchell—was taken with Berry's poise and looks. Mitchell suggested that the beauty queen might have a future walking the runways of the fashion world. It sounded glamorous, and Halle decided to give modeling a try. She would discover that it was not all it was cracked up to be.

Chapter 3

Life as a "Human Coat Hanger"

For twenty-one-year-old Halle Berry, Chicago was an exciting place to live. The city boasts a majestic skyline, an active nightlife, and hordes of young people trying to be successful in the world. Berry found the pace faster than that of her native Cleveland, and sometimes it seemed as if the city was always in a hurry.

The modeling world is hardly glamorous for someone just starting out. Beginning modeling opportunities, like most entry-level jobs in entertainment or the arts, do not pay well. Berry's height also put her at a disadvantage. Runway models for live fashion shows tend to be at least five feet, ten inches tall. Many even top six feet. Berry stands somewhere between five feet six and five feet seven, too short for runway work.

Twenty-one-year-old Halle Berry dreamed of
making it big in the fast-paced city of Chicago.

However, Berry was well suited for modeling clothing in newspaper, magazine, and catalog advertisements, where height did not matter. Berry landed some good jobs for the Land's End clothing catalog and in ads for the department stores Marshall Fields and Lord & Taylor.

Chicago is an expensive city in which to live, and Berry was not making enough money from modeling to have her own place. She tried to make ends meet by sharing a one-bedroom apartment with several roommates. It was often crammed with extra people, too—other young models camped out on the floor of the apartment.

Berry and her roommates found a convenient way to save money on meals. Several of the bars in the neighborhood put out free food, such as barbecued chicken wings, for their customers. These appetizers often served as dinner for the young women.

Gradually, Berry got better-paying modeling jobs. Tired of living in the crowded apartment, she moved into a new one, which she shared with a model named Susan. One day, Berry had to travel to Milwaukee, ninety minutes away, for a photo shoot. When she returned home, she was in for a shock. Susan had moved out.

This left Berry with a huge problem. The monthly rent for the apartment was $1,300, and she could not afford to pay the entire bill on her own. Yet she did not want to lose the apartment.

Berry's first impulse was to call her mother. After all, Judith Berry had always been supportive through rough moments. But instead of lending Halle money, Judith gave her daughter a stern lecture. The modeling business is a difficult one, she said. Halle would have to get used to dealing with tough situations. She told her daughter it was time to figure a way out of the mess on her own.

Halle was enraged by her mother's attitude.[1] To pay her bills, she had to take even more modeling work, as well as a second job as a waitress. In her little free time, Berry took acting classes. Years later, she came to understand that her mother had done the right thing. Berry explained, "She made me realize I had to either sink or swim.

From that moment forward, I became independent."[2] Her independence had limits, however. Berry's boyfriend in Chicago, a dentist named John Ronan, helped out when she was strapped for cash.[3]

Berry did not know it at the time, but a woman she had met during her beauty-pageant days was about to do her a big favor. The woman knew a New York City talent manager, Vincent Cirrincione, and told him about Berry.

In 1989, Cirrincione called Berry at her Chicago apartment and invited her to submit a videotape of her work. Berry sent a tape of herself onstage doing a monologue. Impressed, Cirrincione suggested that Berry travel to New York to meet him and possibly land more work. Just three months later, Berry found herself moving to New York City.

A short time later, Cirrincione was stunned to discover that Berry had cut her long, thick hair into a sassy, short-cropped hairdo. In a business that seemed to be ruled by women with long, flowing hair, he thought Berry had made a huge mistake. Cirrincione later recalled, "I sent her out for a . . . commercial and she showed up having cut off all her long hair. I looked at that short crop and said, 'Well, there goes your commercial career.' And she said, 'That's not why I'm here.'"[4]

By then, Berry's heart was set on becoming an actress. She had become disenchanted with modeling: "I hated it and didn't want to do it. There had to be a better way to make a buck! It was the most boring work I ever did. Not being able to have a say, being a human coat hanger."[5]

Berry had a strategy in cutting her hair short. Many young African-American women trying to carve a career in acting had long, straight hair. Berry wanted a different look. In addition, with her new hairdo, Berry's high cheekbones and beautifully proportioned face would stand out, rather than a mane of thick hair.

Berry's first days in New York City were no more glamorous than her time in Chicago. New York is a more expensive city than Chicago, and Berry spent a few weeks sleeping in a homeless shelter. She also spent some nights at a Young Women's Christian Association (YWCA) dormitory. Then, Cirrincione and his wife, Vera, felt compassion for Berry and allowed her to sleep on the couch in their home. At times, Vera Cirrincione was so concerned about Berry's safety as a young woman in a big city that she accompanied her on auditions.

> By then, Berry's heart was set on becoming an actress.

One audition was for the daytime television soap opera *Days of Our Lives*. This show, a favorite of soap opera fans for decades, is one of the most popular programs of its type. Getting a role on such a legendary program would be a huge opportunity for someone trying to break into the acting business. But it was not to be. Berry was rejected by the *Days of Our Lives* producers.

She also tried out for another television show, an updated version of the 1970s drama *Charlie's Angels*. The stories center on three beautiful former policewomen. They are hired by a man named Charlie to work as detectives, tracking down criminals and solving crimes. Again Berry was not hired. She later said that she believed her background as a beauty-pageant winner and model hurt her because some television producers assumed she was a bubble-headed beauty queen with looks but no talent. As it turned out, *Charlie's Angels 88* never aired on television.

One person who did recognize Berry's talent was Aaron Spelling, producer of such long-running television series as *Dynasty*, *Beverly Hills 90210*, and *Melrose Place*. Spelling was impressed by Berry's auditions and encouraged her to keep trying.

Berry next tried out for a new television program that was to premiere that fall. It was a spin-off—a show based on the characters or plot of an existing series—of a situation comedy called *Who's the Boss?* In an episode of *Who's the Boss?* a character goes to New York on an assignment for her school newspaper. She is supposed to interview a group of women trying to break into modeling. That episode became the basis for a new comedy, called *Living Dolls*, which was centered on the lives of models.

Who could better play the role of a young model than a young woman who actually was a model? The four characters in *Living Dolls* share a crowded apartment, just as Berry had done in Chicago. For Berry, this audition would lead to her first break as an actress. After only a few months of tryouts, she was being hired to play one of the leads in a television series.

In the entertainment business, that is practically overnight success. Many actors spend years auditioning for parts before landing a lead in a movie or television series. Most are never chosen for the top roles. There are actors who do not succeed at all, working as waiters or doing other jobs before giving up entirely. For Berry to get a lead part so soon was highly unusual.

The legendary television producer Aaron Spelling told Berry not to give up.

The six main characters in *Living Dolls* all have distinct personalities. Some critics said the characters were too stereotypical. Berry played Emily Franklin, a serious and brainy woman trying to earn money to pay for medical school. The other models were Caroline, bratty and spoiled; Martha, naïve and innocent; and Charlie, a tough girl from the streets. The two other main characters are Trish, a middle-aged woman who ran the agency that employed the models, and Trish's sixteen-year-old son, Rick, who considered himself the luckiest teenager in the world because he was surrounded by beautiful women.

Like most television programs, *Living Dolls* was videotaped well ahead of being shown on television. One day in the middle of a videotaping session, Berry suddenly collapsed on the set and was rushed to a nearby hospital.

She later said, "When I came to the hospital, they told me I was a diabetic, but I thought I was dying, because all I heard was 'disease.'"[6] She added, "All I heard was that I would have to have shots every day and I could lose my legs."[7] Berry was told she had Type 2 diabetes. Like many people diagnosed with ailments that seem frightening, Berry at first did not want to believe the doctors. She refused to change her lifestyle and continued to eat as she always had. Diabetics must eat a well-controlled diet and get regular exercise. Berry did not alter her exercise routine or her attitudes about living. Before long, she needed to give herself insulin injections. She realized then that her health was too serious to ignore.

> She realized finally that her health was too serious to ignore.

It soon seemed there would be even more stress in her life. *Living Dolls* premiered on Tuesday night, September 26, 1989. The vast majority of television critics had nothing good to

◆◆◆◆◆◆◆◆◆◆◆

Diabetes

Diabetes occurs when one's body does not produce or properly use insulin, a hormone that allows the body to process a sugar called glucose. Glucose is a product of digestion and a source of energy for the body. Common symptoms of diabetes include excess thirst, frequent urination, and increased fatigue. Uncontrolled diabetes can lead to blindness, kidney failure, and severe problems with circulation that can lead to amputation of a foot.

There are two main types of diabetes: Type 1 and Type 2. Type 2 diabetes occurs when the body cannot use insulin properly. Type 1 occurs when the body fails even to produce insulin.

say about the show. They said the scripts were filled with clichés, the acting was stiff, the plots were weak, and the pacing was poor.

Many television programs succeed despite poor reviews. As long as a show attracts enough viewers, it can be a success. But *Living Dolls* would have no such luck. Later in September, the show was moved from Tuesday to Saturday. This new time slot did not draw a larger audience. *Living Dolls* was by all accounts a failure. It did not even last out the year. The last episode aired on December 30, 1989.

The living dolls of *Living Dolls*, from left: Deborah Tucker,
Halle Berry, Allison Elliot, and Leah Remini. Though the show
quickly flopped, Berry's acting career was on the move.

Chapter 4

And Justice for Halle

Not one to give up, Berry kept trying out for parts. In 1991, she landed a role in a night-time serial called *Knots Landing*, playing television production assistant Debbie Porter. *Knots Landing* had been an extremely popular program when it debuted in 1979. However, by 1991 most of the original cast had left, and ratings were not as high as they had been. Even so, the show still had millions of viewers. For Berry, it was an upward career move.

Berry's acting caught the eye of the controversial movie director Spike Lee. Although he stands only five feet five inches tall, Lee is a giant among filmmakers. Lee— himself African-American—first became known in the mid-1980s for directing comedies about African-American life in the United States. Then, in 1989 he gained fame for directing *Do The Right Thing*, a fiery film about race relations.

Millions of *Knots Landing* viewers became exposed
to the face of Halle Berry as Debbie Porter,
pictured here with actor Larry Riley.

In 1990 Lee was casting another movie, to be called *Jungle Fever*. The subject was the difficulty involved in interracial dating. The main plotline was a romance between an Italian-American woman and her boss, a successful African-American architect. Lee contacted Berry to audition for the supporting role of a beautiful homemaker married to a schoolteacher. But Berry had a different idea.

She wanted to play the part of Vivian, a poor and desperate woman addicted to the illegal drug crack cocaine. Lee told her there was no way she could convincingly play that role, because she was too pretty.

Berry later said about a similar role, "I've always had to struggle to prove that I'm more than just a shell. . . . When I auditioned, I heard people say, 'Halle Berry's too beautiful for this role.' I thought to myself: What? *Only unattractive people get hooked on crack?* What a stupid stereotype. Drugs affect everybody."[1]

Berry wanted to prove to both movie insiders and the public that she was more than just a pretty face. She finally persuaded Lee to let her try out for the part of Vivian. Impressed by her talent, Lee hired her.

Playing Vivian was a challenge that Berry did not take lightly. Having spent her teen years in a comfortable suburb, Berry knew nothing about the lives of poverty-stricken drug addicts. To prepare for the role, Berry had one of her costars, Samuel L. Jackson, drive her to some of the poorest neighborhoods in New York City. At one point, she went with a police officer to a crack house—where crack addicts lived and where they sold and used drugs. The police officer gave her a bulletproof vest to wear.

Berry was shocked by what she saw. The conditions were squalid, and people in the neighborhoods were armed with automatic weapons and knives. She was especially disturbed to see children among the drug addicts.

Seeing how addicts live was not enough for Berry. To convincingly play a drug addict, she wanted to live like one. She did not try crack cocaine, but for ten days before the film was shot she did not bathe. She was trying to look and feel as grungy as possible.

The movie's makeup artists painted pimples and sores on the former beauty queen's face, and gave her a messy hairdo. To complete her new look, Berry dressed in tattered clothing. The glamorous actress was gone.

Berry said the role "got me away from that beauty pageant-model stigma, because that's all I had done up until then. My first acting job was playing a model on television. So the movie gave me a chance to show a different side of myself. It also proved the kind of chances I was willing to take."[2]

Jungle Fever was a hit. It made money and was praised by critics. But the same critics had differing views of *Jungle Fever*'s message. Some thought the theme was that it is foolish for people to be disturbed by interracial romance in the face of more important issues such as crime and drugs. Others thought Lee was saying that interracial romances simply do not work, a view Berry did not agree with. Off camera, Berry got into an argument with Spike Lee. "He said my parents divorced because black/white love can never work. I told Spike that that was just his warped and twisted point of view. The reality was that my parents loved each other . . . they split up because of my father's drinking."[3]

"Jungle Fever gave me a chance to show a different side of myself."

By now, Berry had proved that she was a talented and versatile actress. She followed her dark role in *Jungle Fever* with a completely different type of character in the 1991 movie *Strictly Business*.

Unlike *Jungle Fever*, with its heavy-handed message, *Strictly Business* is a lighthearted romantic comedy. *Strictly Business* takes place in the business world, where Berry plays a hip waitress named Natalie. Real estate executive Waymon Tisdale III, played by Joseph C. Phillips, has a crush on Natalie. Yet while Waymon is successful at business, he is shy and awkward around women. A mailroom clerk—Bobby Johnson, played by Tommy Davidson—knows Natalie. So Waymon makes a deal. If Bobby can introduce him to Natalie, Waymon will help Bobby get a job promotion.

As in the past, Berry's skin color became an issue, but with a switch. Berry was originally hired to play Natalie, then let go. Actress A. J. Johnson was brought in to replace her. Costar Joseph C. Phillips said, "The movie's producers and writers were adamant that they wanted a darker skinned girl [than Berry] to play Natalie, and A. J. Johnson is dark skinned. Too often it is only lighter skinned black women who are identified with beauty."[4]

Berry understood the filmmakers' point of view but believed they should have thought it through before hiring her. As it turned out, the producers kept changing

Berry with costars Tommy Davidson, left, and Joseph C. Phillips, center, in *Strictly Business*.

their minds about how Johnson should play Natalie. Phillips said, "They kept wanting her to do something different, like cut her hair or put extensions in her hair. She was getting frustrated."[5] Soon afterward, Johnson was gone, and Berry was rehired.

Phillips said that at the time both he and Berry were struggling actors. They became good friends but never dated. "I would like to think that was because she felt safe with me because I was one of the few men not hitting on her," he said. "She shared some things with me, like she had had a stalker who was threatening her when she was doing *Living Dolls* and they had to close down the set."[6]

Phillips was impressed during the filming of *Strictly Business* with how strongly Berry gets into her roles. Off the set, he observed her extraordinary magnetism: "I have worked with a lot of beautiful women, some I think are prettier than Halle. But Halle constantly drew men's attention. If we were walking together, men were always breaking their necks trying to look at her. . . . If we went into a room and she sat down, before you know it all the men in the room would be gathered around her."[7]

Strictly Business received mixed reviews from movie critics. Several thought it was funny but had a weak plot. Others said that the weak plot overshadowed the funny dialogue. The movie made only a small profit.

Money and reviews aside, the movie was noteworthy for a different reason. Some critics appreciated the movie for showing that the African-American experience extended beyond housing projects into the business world. Phillips said, "I think it was a great message. It was one of the first films in cinematic history that showed black middle-class corporate life. [Other African Americans] have told me the movie was a kind of milestone moment in their lives. They finally had a movie that reflected their lifestyle."[8]

Berry's next movie, *The Last Boy Scout*, tells the story of a down-and-out private detective who teams up with a disgraced former football player to find a murderer. An action-adventure flick, *The Last Boy Scout* is filled with car crashes and explosions. While some movies can get away with excess violence to further the plot and add suspense, that was not the case with *The Last Boy Scout*. Most critics hated it, and the movie made little money. Berry played the former football player's lowlife girlfriend.

After that, Berry took a chance with another romantic comedy. In *Boomerang*, which came out in 1992, Berry plays Angela Lewis, the assistant to a woman business executive named Jackie Broyer. Angela dates her boss's former boyfriend, the successful businessman Marcus Graham, played by the famous comedian/actor Eddie Murphy. Marcus is a popular man, accustomed to breaking women's hearts. But in a reversal, Jackie breaks Marcus's heart. Marcus then decides to date Jackie's assistant, Angela, who is a sweet and sincere person.

It was not easy for Berry to get the role of Angela. Eddie Murphy is a top star, and his contract gave him final approval of the cast. Even though she was by now a well-known actress with several strong performances under her belt, Berry had to audition for the part. She did a powerful scene in which Angela gets tired of Marcus's attitude and angrily breaks up with him. Murphy was so impressed that he gave her the part on the spot. Others were waiting to audition, but Murphy told producer Warrington Hudlin to send them all home.

While many famous actors are known for thinking highly of themselves and not mingling with others on the movie set, Berry came across as very friendly, with her feet on the ground. Hudlin said that many actors do not pay attention to the workers who do the less glamorous, behind-the-scenes jobs in movies. He said that Berry "would eat with the crew, she would sit down with the grips [stagehands whose job it is to move scenery] and gaffers [electricians]. She is such a regular, down-to-earth accessible person. It just shocked me how sweet she was. . . . But then you meet her mother and she's so sweet and down-to-earth you go, okay, that's where it came from."[9]

Boomerang made a profit but received mixed reviews. Even though the theme of *Boomerang* was not controversial like that of *Jungle Fever*, the movie still got people arguing. Several critics had trouble accepting a movie with African-American characters who were not inner-city residents.

Some condemned the movie for being unrealistic, and even reverse racist, by having very few white characters. In response, Murphy wrote a guest column in the *Los Angeles Times*, blasting some white people for not accepting that African Americans can be wealthy and successful.

After *Boomerang*, life was filled with opportunity for Berry. In 1992, she heard about *Queen*, a miniseries that was about to be filmed for television. *Queen* was written by Alex Haley, the author of a book named *Roots*. In *Roots* Haley tells the story of his ancestors from their lives in Africa, through decades of slavery, and ending with the onset of the Civil War. The title refers to Haley's ancestors—who are the roots of his family tree. Haley had spent twelve years researching and writing *Roots*.

As a TV miniseries, *Roots* was a tremendous success. About 100 million people, or just a little under half the population of the United States, watched the final episode on January 30, 1977.[10]

The miniseries *Roots* was followed in February 1979 by a sequel, *Roots: The Next Generation*. This miniseries told the Haley family story from 1862 to the present. *Roots: The Next Generation* ran for seven straight nights.

In the 1980s, Haley decided to write a book based on another side of his family history. Haley's paternal grandmother, Queen, was the daughter of a white plantation owner and an African-American slave. This new book would be about her life and would be titled, simply, *Queen*.

The Miniseries *Roots*

Entertainment television series are regularly scheduled programs featuring the same cast of characters in the same setting. Until 1977, one thing was fairly standard: With few exceptions, most new series episodes were televised once a week.

Television producer David L. Wolper changed that. He devised the idea of a series that would be aired on eight consecutive nights. It was a historical drama called *Roots*, based on the book by Alex Haley. Television executives thought *Roots* would be watched by few people. Instead, when it ran in January 1977, it drew more viewers than any entertainment program up to that time. A new kind of TV program was born—the miniseries.

When the book *Roots* was published, Alex Haley knew modest fame. The TV miniseries *Roots* launched him into superstardom and made television history.

Haley died of a heart attack on February 10, 1992, before he had finished the book. A screenplay for *Queen*, based on Haley's unfinished manuscript, was crafted by screenwriter David Stevens. Much of the story focuses on Queen's sad life as a mixed-race woman trying to fit into white society. At one point, she tries passing as white. Later in the story, she is beaten by a white lover when he finds out about her African background.

As soon as Berry heard about the role, she wanted to play Queen. She related to this story about a woman who was half black and half white and had trouble fitting in. Berry said, "I've dealt with some of the problems that Queen faced, on a different scale."[11]

Berry was not being considered for the film, so she went out of her way to audition for it. In many cases, movie and television producers pay the airfare for actors they recruit for parts. Berry wanted the part so much that she willingly paid her own airfare. She also paid her own hotel costs. On top of that, she paid the expenses of a makeup artist as well as the overtime hours the crew had to work during her tryout.

Berry took a gamble and it worked. *Queen*'s producer, Mark Wolper, said he was "blown away" by her audition.[12] She was cast in the title role, as Queen.

The filming was tough. Most of *Queen* was shot in 1992 during the stifling heat of a South Carolina summer. During the shooting, Berry fell off a horse and injured her tailbone. Production was stopped for two weeks. Because the filming was on a tight schedule, Berry was given painkillers to make it possible for her to work. Still, some days the pain was so bad that she was driven to the set in an ambulance.

On top of that, Berry spent four hours every day in makeup. Her character ages from a fifteen-year-old girl in the beginning of the story to a seventy-two-year-old woman at its end. Makeup was applied daily to make Berry look old. Dyes were applied to darken her teeth. In addition, her character is repeatedly abused, which meant that Berry was often slapped. Berry said, "After the horseback accident it was a challenge just to walk. So, after that accident, I really can't be honest about what was hard because everything was hard after that."[13]

People who knew Berry only as a movie star did not know that her personal life was a mess beyond the horse-back riding injury. Female fans jealous of her beauty might have been less envious had they known that her looks and charm did not help her find a boyfriend who was good to her. Somewhere around this time, she got into an argument with a boyfriend who hit her so hard that he broke her left eardrum. "I have no hearing there," she said.[14] Berry has never publicly named the man, but has said he is a "well-known" person in the movie industry.[15]

> As soon as Berry heard about the role, she wanted to play Queen.

Berry connected with the tragedy of Queen,
a mixed-race woman trying to fit into society.

After she split with him, Berry fell into another painful relationship. She confesses, "I wasn't hit like in the other one, but I was mentally abused. . . . I found out he stole my Rolex watch, my diamond earrings. He was living in my house and I came home one day and he'd packed up everything and was gone with all my valuables. And I had given this man everything. I don't even want to go into all of it because I make myself feel stupid when I discuss all the dumb things I did."

She added, "But I didn't do it out of stupidity. I knew what I was doing and I knew the money that I was giving to help him out. But I thought if I can help somebody, then I want to."[16]

One day during a break in the filming of *Queen*, Berry was watching a celebrity baseball game on the cable television network MTV. One athlete she noticed was Atlanta Braves outfielder David Justice. "He seemed like a prince with this gorgeous big smile and massive shoulders," she said.[17]

By coincidence, a journalist who interviewed Berry just a few weeks later happened to be a friend of Justice's. During the interview, the journalist told Berry that Justice was a big fan of hers and wanted an autograph. Berry gave him not only her autograph but her telephone number, too. When Justice called soon afterward, their first conversation lasted four hours. The movie star and the star athlete dated for six months. They were married on New Year's Day, 1993, at his home in Atlanta.

Chapter 5

Of Cavemen and Kings

I t seemed as if Halle Berry had found her Prince Charming in this popular ballplayer. They were both famous and highly regarded in their fields. They had similar backgrounds. Like Berry, Justice had excelled in school. He hardly fit the stereotype of a dumb athlete. Justice was such a good student that he had skipped seventh and eighth grades and graduated from high school at sixteen.

Also like Berry, Justice had grown up in a single-parent home with his mother. His parents split up when he was four, the same age as Berry when her father left. Both Berry and Justice grew up with loving mothers. Justice even had his mother's name, Nettie, tattooed on his arm. Berry said, "A man who loves his mother will love me too."[1]

The celebrity couple Halle Berry and
David Justice seemed to have it all.

As for Justice, he told a reporter shortly after they were married, "I tell Halle, 'I thank God every day for giving you to me.'"[2] The two had homes in Los Angeles and Atlanta, so they could each have a place to live near their respective work.

Meanwhile, *Queen* was televised in February 1993. Since the role was so personal for Berry, she hoped the miniseries would be well received. As with many of her projects, there was a wide range of reviews. The majority of critics thought *Queen* seemed more like a soap opera and had less dramatic punch than the original *Roots* miniseries.

However, most reviews of Berry's performance were positive. *Time* magazine's film critic Richard Zoglin wrote, "*Queen* has poignant moments, thanks largely to Halle Berry's delicate, deeply felt performance in the title role."[3]

Berry had no trouble getting more work. She had three movies released in 1993. In CB4, a spoof of rap music, Berry played herself. The movie follows the adventures of a fictional rap trio called Cell Block 4, or CB4. Onstage, the members of CB4 act like hardened criminals from the inner city's mean streets. But offstage, the rappers are actually clean-living and kind young men from loving homes in friendly neighborhoods.

Another of Berry's 1993 movies was the adventure comedy *Father Hood*. Patrick Swayze stars as a small-time criminal who bonds with a daughter he once placed in a foster home. Berry costars as reporter Kathleen Mercer. Berry's part was small but noteworthy because it was her first movie role in which her race was not a factor.

Finally, Berry costarred in *The Program*. This movie about college football was hardly a rah-rah look at college sports. The players' problems include steroid use, alcohol abuse, and illegal drug use. As a professional athlete, Berry's husband, David Justice, did not like the way drugs and alcohol dominated the players' lives. Justice stated, "Nobody that I know, that we are friends with, is that way. They wouldn't be friends of ours because we don't live that way."[4]

Berry with Omar Epps, right, and Al Wiggins, left, in *The Program*.

Berry's character is a classy, well-educated woman named Autumn Haley. Autumn is hired to tutor a running-back named Darnell Jefferson (played by Omar Epps) from a poor neighborhood. Autumn gradually learns that while Darnell might have grown up on dangerous streets, he is smart and wants to better himself.

While these movies kept Berry busy and earned her money, none was a hit or received rave reviews. Critics wrote that *CB4* had a few funny lines but lacked humor overall. Many rap music fans disagreed, saying the jokes went over the heads of white critics. Movie reviewers thought *The Program* seemed contrived and the characters were not well developed. They saved their worst reviews for *Father Hood*, which most considered a total failure. Berry's performances, however, were sometimes noted as the highlights of the films.

Berry was reaching the point where she could pick and choose her roles. Even so, she was frustrated because she often found that agents (the people who represent actors and help get them parts) saw her mainly as an African-American actress rather than an actress who happened to be African-American. Berry is proud of her heritage, but she does not want to be stereotyped and limited in the roles she can play.

Berry explained, "I still have to convince agents they should send me out for the next level of scripts. I don't want to abandon black filmmakers but I don't want to keep doing 'girls in the hood' either. I look at films like *You've Got Mail* and think: 'I could have played that role.' But black women don't even get a reading."[5] *You've Got Mail* was a successful romantic comedy starring Tom Hanks and Meg Ryan.

Still, even seasoned actors cannot predict the next hit film. Berry was offered a chance to star in an action thriller called *Speed*. The plot revolved around a city bus that had been rigged with a bomb. The driver must maintain a speed of at least fifty miles per hour or the bomb will explode. Berry could have played the courageous bus driver.

However, it was the first movie for director Jan De Bont, which made the film a risky project for an established actor. Berry rejected the offer, and the part went to Sandra Bullock. *Speed* became one of the biggest hits of 1994 and launched Bullock into stardom.

Despite her growing fame, Berry still found herself encountering racism. All celebrities are used to dealing with interruptions when out in public, though there are times when it is especially inconvenient. One day Halle and David were eating in a restaurant when a woman came over to their table and asked for an autograph. The couple said that it was not a good time

> Berry is proud of her heritage, but she does not want to be stereotyped in the roles she can play.

and asked her to come back a little later. The woman lashed out with a racial insult. Berry said, "I didn't think that still happened. That was a rude awakening."[6]

In the fall of each year, the National Academy of Television Arts and Sciences gives out the Emmy Awards. The Emmys are television's version of the movie industry's Academy Awards. They honor outstanding work in television programs of the previous year.

Berry was very proud of her performance in *Queen*. Unfortunately, she was not nominated for an Emmy. Ann-Margret was nominated for outstanding supporting

The NAACP Image Awards

The NAACP Image Awards are presented annually to African Americans who are positive role models. The awards are given to people in the arts for their performances or their devotion to social justice.

The NAACP has expressed concern about the portrayal of African Americans in the media ever since 1915, when the group protested the movie *Birth of a Nation*. The movie, a big hit, depicted African Americans as savages.

The NAACP Image Awards ceremony is televised live across the nation every year.

actress for *Queen*, but the only Emmy awarded to the show was in the best hairstyling category.

However, *Queen* did receive recognition from one of the United States's oldest and most well respected African-American civil-rights groups. The NAACP—National Association for the Advancement of Colored People—honored Berry with an Image Award. She won in the category of best lead actress in a television movie or miniseries.

The year 1993 ended on a sour note. In December, Berry's old boyfriend in Chicago, the dentist John Ronan, sued Berry in a United States District Court for $80,000.[7] Ronan said that when they were dating he had lent Berry money to help her meet expenses as she built a modeling career. Now he wanted his money back. Because Berry is a celebrity, the lawsuit made national news.

To add to Berry's embarrass-ment, Ronan sold personal stories about her to a tabloid newspaper. Many journalists and celebrities accuse the tabloids of printing gossip without checking to see if it is true. Berry insisted that the stories were completely false.[8] She also said Ronan had given her money and gifts, including expensive vacations in Las Vegas and Hawaii. She said they were not loans but presents, like those given by many men to their girlfriends. Berry commented, "The only thing I'm guilty of is taking from a man who wanted to give. Being a young girl without two nickels to rub together, it was very easy to take and not ask questions. You know the phrase 'a woman scorned'? This is a man scorned."[9]

Berry said one of her main concerns was what her husband would think. But he was very understanding. She stated, "He said, 'Baby, don't even worry. This guy can't touch you.' He was so supportive, so loving."[10]

Yet there were stresses in the marriage. Halle's and David's work schedules often kept them apart. In early 1994, Berry was in Africa filming the television movie *Solomon and Sheba*. The couple's long distance bill for the first month she was in Africa totaled $4,500.[11]

Then, when Justice hit the home run that won the World Series for the Braves in October 1995, Berry was three thousand miles away filming a movie in Seattle, Washington. Berry had to watch the most important game of her husband's career on television.

Although Berry had never liked baseball, she tried to attend his home games. She learned the rules of the game and kept score. But after a while, she had to stop going to the Braves games. As a celebrity, she often drew a lot of attention, which caused disturbances in the stands.

In 1994, Berry talked about being part of a celebrity marriage: "Our biggest problem has been dealing with not being together. We also have to deal with the public, with the rumors. Sometimes we find ourselves in big arguments over some rumor somebody started, someone we don't even know. Eventually we realize that we're giving these people too much power. Then we get back to what's real."[12]

Meanwhile, Berry continued to fight Ronan's lawsuit. She had an option to settle the lawsuit out of court. That would consist of their lawyers' working out a compromise, rather than having a judge render a decision. More than likely, a settlement would have called for Berry to pay Ronan a portion of the money he was demanding. But for Berry, settling was not an option. Settling would imply she was guilty. Berry insisted she was innocent, and she wanted her name to be cleared.

Despite her personal problems, Berry had her career to keep her busy. She heard that a movie was going to be made based on an old television cartoon, *The Flintstones*, about a Stone Age family living in the prehistoric suburban town of Bedrock. Rather than be animated, the movie would feature live actors.

A new character created for the movie was a pretty secretary named Sharon Stone. She uses her looks and charm to try to lure Fred into an illegal money-making scheme. The actress Sharon Stone often plays that kind of role. The director of *The Flintstones*, Brian Levant, thought it would be funny if the real Sharon Stone played the character Sharon Stone. However, the actress was not interested in the part.

So Berry decided to audition for it. She joked with Levant, suggesting that it was about time black people lived in Bedrock. Levant agreed: Considering that early humans lived in Africa, there should be blacks in Bedrock. Berry had another reason for trying out. She said, "I really pushed for the part. It was important to me that a black woman be seen as the object of desire."[13]

Levant's wish to integrate Bedrock helped Berry get the part, but both Levant and the movie's producer, Steven Spielberg, were also impressed with her powerful audition. Berry's fellow actors asked why she would want to go from serious roles such as Queen to playing a Stone Age secretary in a children's movie. Berry said, "I guess I take on such varied parts because I don't want to be pigeonholed. I don't want people to think they know who I am or what I'm capable of. I feel that I should be the only one who determines that."[14]

Critics were not kind to *The Flintstones*. Most considered the movie a failure, saying the acting was fine

Halle Berry and Kyle MacLachlan in *The Flintstones*.

but the script was weak. On the other hand, audiences across the world saw the movie in droves, and it made a huge profit. It was the first time Berry had a role in a movie that earned more than $100 million.[15]

There was more good news for Berry in 1994. In October, a judge threw out John Ronan's lawsuit. The court said Ronan had not proved that any of the money or gifts he gave to Berry were meant to be loans. Although it cost her more than $50,000 in lawyers' fees, Berry had made the right decision not to settle the case out of court.[16] Berry said, "I work hard for my money and I can't think of a better way to spend it than to protect my character."[17]

Berry's next television movie, *Solomon and Sheba*, aired on the Showtime pay cable television network on February 26, 1995. Berry had chosen her role carefully. The Biblical Queen of Sheba was Ethiopian, but when a movie based on the same story was released in 1959 the queen was played by the white actress Gina Lollobrigida. Of course, in 1959 a movie depicting an interracial

The Flintstones

The Flintstones was first televised on Friday evening, September 30, 1960. Unlike most cartoons in those days, *The Flintstones* drew viewers of all ages. Children laughed at the antics of Fred and Wilma Flintstone and their neighbors Barney and Betty Rubble. Adults saw the show as a satire about modern suburban life. Fred was a construction worker who drove a convertible with an animal-skin top and stone wheels. Wilma gossiped on a telephone made from an animal horn. The daily newspaper was carved onto a stone tablet. The last original episode of *The Flintstones* was televised in 1966, but spin-offs and specials were aired well into the 1990s.

relationship, even one based on the Bible, would have been a financial failure. Theaters throughout the southern United States would never have shown it. By the mid-1990s, Berry thought times had changed, and it was unrealistic for a white woman to portray an Ethiopian queen. It was very important to her that she play the part.

Even though Berry had said she wanted to get away from "girl in the hood" movies, she did take one more: a role as a crack cocaine addict in the 1995 movie *Losing Isaiah*. Again, she did so because of a personal reason. The plot focused on a white couple raising an African-American child. The movie questioned whether it was better for an African-American child to be raised by secure, loving white parents or a single African-American mother with a troubled past.

In *Losing Isaiah*, a drug addict named Khalia Richards abandons her baby son, Isaiah, who is rescued by a white social worker, played by Jessica Lange. The social worker and her husband legally adopt Isaiah. Meanwhile, Khalia tries to better herself. She gets treatment for her drug addiction, so she is no longer dependent on cocaine. She also gets a job with a steady income. Several years after she abandoned Isaiah, Khalia wants him back. Khalia says it is better for an African-American child to grow up with a struggling single African-American parent than with two middle-class white parents.

Berry and Jessica Lange in *Losing Isaiah*. Berry had strong feelings about the complex issues of race and raising children in this film.

Around the time *Losing Isaiah* was released, Berry said, "I could imagine my mother being told she couldn't raise me because of the color of her skin. When you love a child, it doesn't matter what color your skin is. What matters is that a black child is taught about his history and culture and is prepared for the racism he'll face. To shelter him and let him grow up in a fantasy world where everyone is equal is to do him a big disservice. But I know it can be done because my mother did it."[18]

Chapter 6

In the
Public Eye

ven though Berry had starred and costarred in
several films and television shows, she had never
had a breakout movie. None of her successes
made her stand out as a superstar.

Losing Isaiah lost money, and the reviews were generally not good. Most critics blamed the script. While the
screenwriter wanted to tell a noble and thoughtful story,
reviewers said the characters were weak and stereotyped.
They also thought the story was forced and contrived.

Some of the critics' few compliments went to the female
leads, Jessica Lange and Halle Berry. Although the two are
from different backgrounds, they share common experiences. Both had made the transition from modeling to
acting. Each had proved that she could handle challenging
roles. Yet Berry still faced some of the same criticisms she

had endured in the past. Regarding *Losing Isaiah*, one critic wondered if there could realistically be "a poor, unmarried, reformed crackhead as pretty as Halle Berry."[1]

Berry continued to keep busy. In March 1996 one of the world's largest cosmetic companies, Revlon, announced that Berry would be its spokesmodel. That means she would be featured in all kinds of advertisements for Revlon products. Berry's predecessor, Cindy Crawford, has long been regarded as one of the world's most beautiful women. Berry would be the first African-American woman to serve as a Revlon spokesmodel. She believed that breaking the racial barrier was long overdue. "When I was growing up," she said, "it was hard to find black images of beauty. Things are changing and I want to be part of it."[2]

The Revlon contract was the high point in what was otherwise a tough year. Berry appeared in four very different films, none noteworthy. One was the comedy *Girl 6*, in which she had a small role as herself. The director was Spike Lee, the same moviemaker who had given her a break five years earlier in *Jungle Fever*. Another project for Berry was *Race the Sun*, the first movie in which she received top billing. That means her name was listed first in the credits. It was an inspirational movie based on a true story. Berry played Sandra Beecher, a teacher at a high school in a poor neighborhood in Hawaii. She helps her discouraged students build a solar-powered car and compete in a race against teams from around the world.

Revlon spokesmodel Halle Berry is ready for the
12th annual Revlon fundraiser to fight women's cancers.

Berry's third movie of 1996 was a suspense thriller, *The Rich Man's Wife*. Her character, Josie Potenza, is an unhappy woman accused of murdering her rich husband. Berry was excited about playing the lead in another movie in which her race was not relevant to the plot, but she was also nervous: "It's satisfying, but I'm also scared to death! I'd be lying if I said that [I] didn't feel pressure, but I know why I'm doing what I'm doing, and I'm really doing this because I love to act. And I love to be in front of the camera."[3] *The Rich Man's Wife* did not make a splash with critics or with moviegoers, though Berry's performance garnered some positive feedback. This film, like *Girl 6* and *Race the Sun*, was not a high point in her career.

> "When I was growing up, it was hard to find black images of beauty. Things are changing and I want to be part of it."

Executive Decision was Berry's only hit movie in 1996. It is an action-adventure story about Arab terrorists who highjack an airplane and threaten to blow it up over Washington, D.C. Berry plays a courageous flight atten- dant who uses her brains and strong will to help law enforcement authorities capture the terrorists. Critics generally agreed that *Executive Decision* was a riveting movie filled with thrills and tense moments. But in a switch from poorly received movies in which Berry stood out, the critics were not as kind to Berry this time. Many thought her acting performance was limited. However, *Executive Decision* was the only one of Berry's four movies in 1996 that drew fairly large audiences.

Behind the scenes, Berry was working on a pet project. She wanted to make a movie about Dorothy Dandridge. Berry had felt a special connection with the actress ever since she learned that she and Dandridge were born forty-six years apart in the same Cleveland hospital. Berry thought Dandridge's troubled life would make a fascinating movie subject. She met with major movie studio executives but received one rejection after another. The answer was almost always the same: Dandridge might interest African Americans, but her story would never draw enough white moviegoers to make the movie financially successful.

While Berry's career seemed to be at a standstill, her personal situation was worse. Her marriage was crumbling. The couple's mutual fame was a problem. Berry explained, "I knew the reality of being public people and both of us having such demanding careers had started to take its toll on our relationship."[4]

Since Berry and Justice were both celebrities, their divorce became a major news item. Some of the most personal details of their private lives became public knowledge. For Berry, the pain of the divorce brought back childhood memories and spurred her to take a surprising step. "The day I filed for a divorce from David, I telephoned my father," she said. "I had to track him down because

Dorothy Dandridge

Dorothy Dandridge was a trailblazing African-American actress. Her acting and singing talents won her varied roles at a time when most African Americans were stereotyped into playing servants. Ironically, even when Dandridge performed in some of the nation's finest hotel nightclubs, segregation laws banned her from staying overnight in the same hotels. In 1954, she was nominated for an Academy Award for best actress for the movie *Carmen Jones*. She was the first African-American actress to receive that honor. Dandridge died tragically at forty-two. Some say she committed suicide while others believe her death was due to an accidental drug overdose.

Dorothy Dandridge's talent, success, and beauty did not shield her from the ugliness of racial discrimination.

I hadn't talked with him in years. I was filled with pain and rage. I got him on the phone and I unleashed all this anger. . . . I told him how much he had hurt me by abandoning our family, by not being in my life when I was a child. At the end of the conversation, I think he said, 'I'm sorry.'"[5]

That conversation might have helped Berry feel better for a little while, but it did not stop the pain of a messy divorce. Berry put on a brave face in public, but at one point the agony became so severe that Berry considered committing suicide. "For two or three hours, I just cried and cried," she said. "I thought, 'I can't face it.' I think that's the weakest I have ever been in my life. That's what the breakup of my marriage did to me. It took away my self-esteem. It beat me down to the lowest of lows—the gum on the bottom of David's shoe, that's what I felt like."[6]

What made Berry decide to stay alive? On the television show *Larry King Live*, she said, "When I was sitting there, really—with all my heart, wanting to end my life. I thought of my mother and I thought, Wow. How unfair. I would break her heart. My heart's broken and I'm going to kill myself. I would break her heart. I would break her heart and I——"

Larry King interrupted, saying, "Someone once said suicide is a selfish act."

Berry immediately answered: "It is. And it's cowardly. It was harder for me to get out of that car and deal with my pain than to end it. You're right."[7]

Berry said in 1997 that she had healed and "wouldn't even think about" suicide. "I know it sounds cliché, but you have to find a way to hold on because time really does heal all wounds."[8]

In 1997, Berry put her pain behind her and went back to making movies. She was offered one of the two lead roles in B*A*P*S, a comedy written, produced, and directed by African Americans. The title is an acronym for "Black American princesses." Berry and costar Natalie Desselle play young women from Georgia who move to Los Angeles to try and make it big as dancers in a rap video. The trouble is that the two women are clueless. They dress in poor taste. Their fingernails are too long, their earrings are huge, and Berry's character's hair is almost ivory in color. A twist in the plot occurs when the women become involved in a scam involving a millionaire on his death bed.

The critics were as unkind to B*A*P*S as they were to *The Rich Man's Wife*. Most thought it was poorly made and some felt it was insulting to African Americans. It was also a disaster financially. Berry did not care about the reaction. She saw B*A*P*S as a means of helping her out of the blues. Doing this lighthearted movie provided a distraction from her problems.[9]

A few years later, in 2003, after Berry had won the Academy Award, she referred to B*A*P*S as a "mindless

> Berry put on a brave face in public, but for a while the agony was terrible.

comedy" and said she took the part because she needed the money. "And to this day," she said, "people still come up to me and ask, 'Why did you do that movie?' . . . People think actors can just sit back and wait for the perfect movie, but who pays the bills in the interim? Fairies don't come down and put money under your pillow. The more successful you become, the more financial responsibilities you have. You want to help out family members who are less fortunate than you are. So you can

The goofball comedy *B*A*P*S* was not a high point
in Berry's career. At left is her costar, Natalie Desselle.

say, 'Okay, I'll do that to help out Uncle Johnny.' That's what family is. That's what family does."[10]

It was also around that time that she met a handsome singer named Eric Benet. Both Berry and Benet said they started as friends long before they began dating. Although Benet was well known among rhythm-and-blues fans, he was not nearly as famous as Berry. When they were seen together in public as a couple, gossip columnists would refer to them as a Hollywood star and an aspiring singer. Benet said that at first it was weird, but he got used to it.

Berry was a Hollywood star, but she had not yet found a role that would make her a superstar. She took a risk in 1998 by appearing in another television miniseries, *The Wedding*. Some movie actors consider it a step down in their career to appear on television. It is true that Berry had done the made-for-television movies *Queen* and *Solomon and Sheba* in the past. But that was before she had so many Hollywood films under her belt.

Berry felt it was worth taking a chance on *The Wedding*. It was being produced by the well-known and powerful African-American talk show host and businesswoman Oprah Winfrey. With Winfrey's name in the title—*Oprah Winfrey Presents: The Wedding*—the project gained respect. Winfrey would not attach her name to a movie if she did not consider it a top-quality product.

The miniseries takes place in the 1950s. Berry's character—a young, wealthy African-American woman named Shelby Coles—is about to marry a white jazz pianist named Meade Howell. In a switch from many plots, the African-American Coles family is rich and the white Howells are poor. In that period of open prejudice, the Coles parents encourage their daughter to marry a white man. While the wedding is being planned, an African-American single father named Lute McNeil falls in love with Shelby. Lute tries to persuade Shelby to marry him instead of Meade. In another break from clichéd plots, Shelby's family wants her to reject Lute and marry her white fiancé. The miniseries aired in February 1998.

Berry noted, "On the surface this could seem like a story of racial issues, but what it's really about is love. It's about family. It's about people accepting one another for who they are, not for the color of their skin, or how much money they have, or how educated they are."[11]

The miniseries did not match the success of *Queen* five years earlier, but Berry's acting did merit an Image Award nomination from the NAACP. Perhaps an even bigger benefit *The Wedding* provided to Berry was the birth of a friendship with Oprah Winfrey. Berry looked up to Winfrey as a mentor, and Winfrey said that she began to think of Berry as a kid sister.

Berry starred in two movies in 1998. One was *Why Do Fools Fall in Love*, the story of the popular 1950s African-American teen singer Frankie Lymon and his troubled personal life. Berry played one of Lymon's former wives.

Berry was ready to give romance another chance with singer Eric Benet.

She received top billing even though Lymon, played by Larenz Tate, was the lead character. Many critics thought the plot was weak, and the movie did not draw much of an audience.

Berry's other 1998 movie was *Bulworth*, a dark satire about politics and business. The movie stars acting legend Warren Beatty as politician Jay Billington Bulworth, a liberal Democrat from California. Bulworth has tried to champion the causes of poor and powerless people. However, he has taken donations from big corporations to raise the money needed to run for the Senate.

The businesses did not give Bulworth money just to be nice. They expected something in return—a promise that Bulworth will vote for laws that will help them. Much of what those big companies want goes against Bulworth's views. Yet without their financial help, he cannot win the election. Once elected, Senator Bulworth keeps his promise, but voting against his conscience leaves him feeling guilty.

Disgusted with the hypocrite he has become, Bulworth decides he cannot live with himself. He hires a hit man—or paid murderer—to kill him. Bulworth does not know that he has actually hired a woman, Nina, played by Berry.

What makes *Bulworth* a biting satire is the way the senator behaves after he has hired someone to kill him. Since he expects to die soon, he no longer worries about being reelected. He says in public what he really thinks,

Halle Berry and Warren Beatty became good friends
after starring together in *Bulworth*, above.

not what people want to hear. Much of it is offensive. Bulworth is especially hard on minorities, especially Jews and African Americans.

While speaking at an African-American church in south central Los Angeles, Bulworth meets and falls in love with Nina, not knowing she is the person out to kill him. The two form a bond, and through Nina's companionship, Bulworth gets a real look at inner-city life.

The movie received very good reviews, and Berry was nominated again for an NAACP Image Award. Yet many African Americans were offended by the satirical dialogue. Berry was stunned by those reactions. She emphasized that the movie was a satire and that actor Warren Beatty is no bigot. Berry urged African Americans to look more at the movie's message about politics and business and less at the specific dialogue.

An offscreen bonus to making *Bulworth* was meeting Warren Beatty, who became an important friend and mentor to Berry. While Berry was not the star of *Bulworth*, she did receive plenty of attention for her role as Nina. Still, it was not the breakout role she had hoped for.

Chapter 7

From Star to Superstar

ne trait that has helped make Halle Berry so successful is her perseverance. After failing to persuade movie studios to take a chance on a Dorothy Dandridge biographical movie, Berry decided to try another outlet—television. The premium cable television network Home Box Office (HBO) is regarded by critics as the source of some of the best programming on television. HBO agreed to make the movie.

Berry served as an executive producer. That means she was partly in charge of overseeing the entire project. She also would play Dandridge. To truly shine in the role and do justice to Dandridge's story, Berry went out of her way to learn everything she could about the former star.

Berry met and interviewed one of Dandridge's best friends, Geri Branton, and Dandridge's manager, Earl Mills.

Halle Berry was both the executive producer and
the star of *Introducing Dorothy Dandridge*.

To help Berry prepare for the role, Mills gave her access to Dandridge's personal papers and possessions. He even permitted her to borrow and try on a gown Dandridge had worn on a television program. It was a perfect fit. Berry has a narrow waist, and the dresses she buys usually need to be taken in. But Dandridge's gown seemed almost tailor-made for Berry. She took it as a sign that she was born to play that role.[1]

Berry summed up her devotion to the role of Dandridge by saying, "Even when Dorothy was happy she was sad. Five years ago when I first wanted to do this role I really wasn't ready for it. But after five years of life, I could relate to her much better."[2]

Strange Incidents

Berry was so absorbed with Dandridge, she said she had brushes with the "supernatural." One day she heard a crackling noise from the den where she kept Dandridge's gown. "When I looked in, I saw this tiny little baby doll dress floating in front of Dorothy's gown. It freaked me out so much I just ran up to my bedroom and curled up in a ball," said Berry. Frightened, she called Dandridge's old friend Geri Branton, who told her, "Honey, I talk to Dottie all the time, and if she is at your house, she means you no harm." Flickering lights, open doors—Berry knew it sounded strange, but the incidents felt very real.[3]

While Berry related to many of Dandridge's struggles, she was saddened by Dandridge's drug-related death at an early age. "In my own life, I am determined to change the ending," Berry promised.[4]

Introducing Dorothy Dandridge was first televised on August 21, 1999. The vast majority of reviews were superb. To top it off, Berry won several awards, including her first major ones outside the African-American community. At the Golden Globe Awards ceremony early in 2000, she was recognized for the "best performance by an actress in a TV movie or miniseries." (The Golden Globes are awarded by the Foreign Press Association in Los Angeles.) After accepting the honor, Berry confessed, "This movie was so personal: Dorothy's struggle was so much my own—to be an African-American actress in Hollywood. Tonight, this said, 'I'm a part of this community and I've been accepted.'"[5]

Later that year, at the prestigious Emmy Awards, she finally earned the statuette that had eluded her for *Queen*. Berry announced, "Wherever Dorothy Dandridge

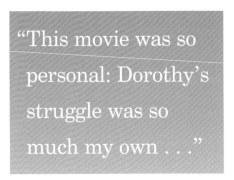

"This movie was so personal: Dorothy's struggle was so much my own . . ."

is right now, she is standing tall and proud. Thank you to my community, who picks me up when I'm down and never, ever lets go."[6]

Halle Berry has expressed thanks for her good fortune many times in more than

Awarded the Golden Globe for her performance in *Introducing Dorothy Dandridge*, Berry celebrates her hard-earned triumph.

just words. She is an active supporter of several charities, especially those she relates to personally. These include the National Juvenile Diabetes Foundation and the Jenesse Center in Los Angeles, which helps victims of domestic violence.

Berry has also helped raise money for Shane's Inspiration, a charity that builds playgrounds for disabled children who find it difficult to play at standard playgrounds. Berry has said that one reason she is so involved

From left: Holly Robinson Peete, Beyoncé Knowles, Halle Berry,
Oprah Winfrey, and Barbara Davis at the sixteenth
annual Carousel of Hope benefit for childhood diabetes.

with the cause is that Shane's Inspiration "builds playgrounds with the hope that disabled children and able-bodied children will be able to play together, which will create more tolerance and acceptance."[7]

In her spare time, Berry enjoys reading and listening to the music of varied performers, such as Norah Jones, Enya, D'Angelo, and Britney Spears. She also enjoys playing with her cats, named Playdough and Spanky, and her Maltese dogs, Polly and Willy, and confesses on her

Web site <http://www.hallewood.com> that her favorite indulgence is butter pecan ice cream.

Yet no matter how much she has tried to avoid it, Berry's life has had a series of dramatic highs and lows. At the same time she was basking in the glory of the success of *Introducing Dorothy Dandridge*, Berry faced a huge public embarrassment.

She had spent the last few months of 1999 and the first six weeks of 2000 working in Canada on *X-Men*, an action/science fiction movie based on the popular comic book series. Her role as the mutant superhero Storm called for her to do a number of stunts. Berry returned home, exhausted, on February 22, 2000.

Early on the morning of February 23, 2000, Berry was driving home from a friend's house in the West Hollywood section of Los Angeles. According to police reports, at about 2:30 A.M. Berry ran a red light and smashed into a car driven by a woman named Hetal Raythatha. The reports said Raythatha's car caught fire and that Berry's car did not stop. Raythatha suffered a broken wrist and had to be pulled from her wrecked car by firefighters.

Berry arrived at her home unaware that she herself had a cut in her forehead almost deep enough to hit bone. When Eric came in after a performance, he saw the gash in her head. She said she did not remember what had happened. He rushed her to a local hospital, where doctors closed the wound with twenty stitches.

In the emergency room, Berry told an off-duty police officer the little she did recall. The next morning, she filed a report with the local sheriff's department.

Accident reports are public documents, and when the local media saw that a celebrity was involved in a car crash, they reported it. The national media picked up the item and broadcast it, too. Soon it was all over the news—famous movie star Halle Berry was involved in a hit-and-run accident in which an innocent person was seriously injured.

Berry said that she suffered amnesia and remembered no major details about the accident. Some people found that hard to believe, though it is medically acknowledged that head injury victims often suffer memory loss. Berry had received a head wound on impact. Some friends thought that weariness from the five-month-long movie shoot she had just completed may have contributed to the accident.

Many people love to gossip about celebrities. Rumors began flying, and jokes at Berry's expense were rampant. On the radio, some deejays twisted the term "Hell on wheels"—often used to describe menacing drivers—to "Helle-on-wheels."[8] At the Oscar Awards in March, comedian Billy Crystal was referring to the famous movie *Driving Miss Daisy* as he quipped on live television, "I just want you all to know they're gonna make a sequel to *Driving Miss Daisy*. But they're going to make it an action film, and they're going to have Halle Berry drive."[9]

Berry, watching the show on television, was horrified. She was going through a personal nightmare, and comedians were joking about it. The next day she called Warren Beatty, her friend from *Bulworth*. Berry later recounted her conversation with Beatty. "I said, 'Did you hear that terrible thing he said about me last night.' And he goes, 'I was there, yeah, I heard it.' And I say, 'That was awful, wasn't it?' And he says, 'No, Halle, all that means is you're famous. Get over it.'"[10]

While Berry tried to develop a thicker skin, she had real life charges to face. On March 31, 2000, she was indicted for leaving the scene of an accident, which is a misdemeanor. The charge carries a maximum sentence of a year in jail. On May 10, 2000, she appeared in the Beverly Hills division of Los Angeles Superior Court and she pleaded "no contest" to the charges. In California, that is the same as a conviction, even though she did not admit guilt. Berry did not have to serve time in jail. Instead, she was put on probation for three years, fined $13,500, and ordered to do two hundred hours of community service.[11]

Berry said to the presiding judge, Charles G. Rubin, "Your honor, I would like the court to know that I have taken this matter

Many people love to gossip about celebrities. Rumors began flying, and jokes at Berry's expense were rampant.

very seriously from the very beginning. I am pleased that this can be resolved."[12]

To reporters, Berry emphasized that the charges of driving under the influence of alcohol or other drugs had been investigated and dismissed—and she was charged not with a felony (hit-and-run) but with a misdemeanor. Still, it was a traumatic ordeal. Raythatha filed a civil lawsuit against Berry, which was settled out of court in May 2001.

The incident did not hurt Berry's career. *X-Men* came out in the summer of 2000 and was a huge success. It was an expensive movie to make, costing $75 million. However, it made more than $150 million in the United States alone.[13]

In *X-Men*, Berry's character, Storm, has the power to control weather and use the wind to fly.

As with *The Flintstones*, some in the business wondered why she chose to costar in a movie based on comic book characters—especially after she had won honors for *Introducing Dorothy Dandridge*. Berry answered that, for one thing, she was not the only big star to appear in *X-Men*. The cast also included the distinguished actors Hugh Jackman, Patrick Stewart, Ian McKellen, and Anna Paquin, who had won an Oscar six years earlier at age twelve. Also, Berry has said many times that she likes playing diverse roles. Finally, Berry did not consider *X-Men* to be simply a comic-book flick. She saw political meaning behind the role, commenting, "The mutants face many of the same obstacles that we do as African-Americans. They're struggling to find equality within a society of non-mutants who fear them out of ignorance. Storm reminds everyone that, if anything is to change, we have to educate people out of their ignorance. That's the substance of who Storm is for me."[14]

In the fall of 2000, Berry was asked by a reporter about her life with boyfriend Eric Benet. Following her messy divorce and the automobile accident, Berry had become very guarded about her personal life. She refused to give the reporter any details. However, a few special friends soon learned that she and Eric were doing very well. The couple sent out a wedding invitation in the form of a message in a bottle. Berry and Benet were married in a private ceremony on January 24, 2001.

Halle Berry and Eric Benet in 2003.

Berry legally adopted Eric's eleven-year-old daughter, India. India's mother had died in an automobile accident in 1993. Berry had grown to love the child, saying, "I'm all she's got as far as a mother goes. It feels as if she's my own; she calls me Mommy."[15] Berry said that she and India enjoyed doing things together, such as shopping and watching *Spongebob Squarepants*, *Lizzie McGuire*, and other television shows.

Berry's next movie, the crime thriller *Swordfish*, was released in June 2001. Unfortunately, her success in the blockbuster *X-Men* did not carry over to *Swordfish*. It was a failure in the eyes of critics, and it earned less money than it cost to make.

Next came *Monster's Ball*, garnering Berry's history-making Academy Award early in 2002. With the Oscar statuette on her mantel and worldwide respect, Berry had finally emerged as a superstar. In her next movie, she broke another racial barrier.

Movies about the fictional international spy James Bond had been made for thirty years. Bond is always portrayed as handsome, sophisticated, successful with women, and always on the right side of justice. His love interests, known as Bond girls, are always as beautiful as he is handsome. So it might not be a total surprise that Berry was asked to act in a James Bond movie.

What made Berry's role notable is that she was the first Oscar winner to play a Bond girl. Also, when Bond movies first were made in the 1960s, the Bond girls were not strong, assertive women. Their main purpose was little more than to look good and cater to James Bond. Because of that, Berry at first was hesitant to take on the role.

She said, "When they first offered me the part I thought what kind of Bond Girl could I be? You know, I really couldn't wrap my brain around it. Then when I

Halle Berry and Billy Bob Thornton in *Monster's Ball*.

As she accepted the Oscar for best actress,
Berry's tears were seen around the world.

read the script I thought, 'Wow, the best kind,' I get to be equal to James Bond. How much fun will that be and how empowering will that be—not only for me as a woman and as an actress, but for other women."[16]

Again, critics questioned her choice of roles. Why would she want to play a Bond girl after winning an Oscar for her role in the serious *Monster's Ball*? Berry explained,

"I see the value in being a part of this movie. It's very different from *Monster's Ball*, but [movies like] *Monster's Ball* are hard to come by. [Bond] is loved around the world. It's a great franchise to be a part of. It's a huge honor."[17]

In *Die Another Day*, Berry is an undercover agent named Jinx. James Bond is played by British actor Pierce Brosnan. Even though Brosnan is fourteen years older than Berry, the two look good as a team. But looking good was not enough for the movie critics, who generally were not kind to *Die Another Day*. Still, the movie drew a big audience and was a financial success.

It was not long after Berry's marriage to Benet that rumors began circulating in tabloid newspapers that the newlyweds were already having troubles. Berry said publicly that those were just ugly rumors and that she, Eric, and India were a happy family of three. She told one reporter, "What you have to understand is that people write bad things about me because it makes the story more interesting. The happy stuff's kind of boring for them."[18]

Berry continued making movies filled with action. She reprised her role as Storm in *X-Men 2*, released in May 2003. Later that year Berry starred in the scary thriller *Gothika*, in which she plays a criminal psychologist who wakes up one day as a patient in her own hospital with no idea why she is there. Soon she learns that she is accused of murdering her husband. As in earlier films, Berry did her own stunts in *Gothika*. During one strenuous scene, she

Berry played opposite Pierce Brosnan in
the James Bond film *Die Another Day.*

broke an arm. After medical treatment, Berry continued working. When the movie came out, she offered *Gothika* audiences a challenge, "See if you can tell when I'm hiding a cast and when I'm acting with both my arms."[19]

While her professional life soared, Berry continued having personal problems. In October 2003 she and Eric separated. Berry then admitted publicly that they had been having "marital problems for some time."[20] In April 2004, the couple officially filed for divorce.

Berry waved to her fans at a screening of *Gothika* in 2003.

Not long afterward, a distressed Halle Berry told Oprah Winfrey that although she looked forward to being in love and having another committed relationship, "I will never marry again."[21]

That summer, Berry also took a chance at playing another comic book character, Catwoman. While she had success with *X-Men*, this movie, titled simply *Catwoman*, was viewed as a failure. It did not make a profit and most critics disliked it. A reviewer for the newspaper *USA Today* said the movie was "like claws on a chalkboard."[22]

Reviews like that did not crush Berry's ability to laugh at herself. Every year a group of movie critics presents the Golden Raspberry Awards, or Razzies. They are given to movies and performances these critics say are the worst of the previous year. The Razzies have their own ceremony, although the "winners" of these insult awards rarely show up.

But Berry said, "The day I heard I won [for *Catwoman*], I thought, 'Oh, great! I'm going to get a nice dress and pick it up myself." Friends told Berry not to go to the Razzies award ceremony, but she said she "never had a second thought about going and making fun of those who made fun of me. It was wonderful. Life is eternal new beginnings."[23]

Berry said she would not accept the Razzies statuette, a golden berry, unless the Razzies presenters engraved her name on it. Then she would keep it in her house.

Berry went back to television in March 2005 when she starred in another Oprah Winfrey project. It was a drama titled *Oprah Winfrey Presents: Their Eyes Were Watching God*, based on a novel written in the 1930s by the famous African-American author Zora Neale Hurston. Berry plays Janie Crawford, who lives through both good and tough times in an African-American community in Florida. The story is inspirational, and in the television viewer ratings for the week, it ranked as number one. Over 17 million people watched the movie, more than any other television show that week.[24]

Many serious critics were impressed by Berry's performance, and the television movie was highly rated, generating additional buzz about Berry's acting talent. The woman who was once barely able to pay her rent could now command a Hollywood salary upward of $20 million per film.

Later that month, in the computer-animated movie *Robots*, movie audiences heard Berry's voice but did not see her face. Berry supplied the voice for an attractive female robot named Cappy. Reviews of the film were mostly positive. One of the nation's best-known movie critics, Roger Ebert, wrote, "Like *Finding Nemo*, this is a movie that is a joy to behold entirely apart from what it is about."[25]

Today, Berry continues living the life of an honored actress. However, she has words of warning for those who think her life is all glamour: "One of the things you learn

When asked about her role as Janie in *Their Eyes Were Watching God*, Berry stated, "I learned a lot, I gave a lot, and I was able to use so many experiences from my own life and sort of channel them through this character."[26]

◆ ◆ ◆ ◆ ◆

in Hollywood is that nothing that's supposed to be 'glamorous' is all that glamorous! You only learn that when you get there. But if I have had a real moment of glamour in my life, it was literally the moment when I won the Oscar. Not the moment when I was sitting there before, or after I walked off the stage. It was only the moment on stage—that was the epitome of glamour! Professionally, I don't think it will ever get any better than that, even if I'm lucky enough to be up there again."[27]

Chronology

1966—Halle Maria Berry is born August 14 in Cleveland, Ohio.

1970—Father, Jerome Berry, moves out of the house and cuts off contact with his family.

1976—Berry, her mother, and her sister move to the Cleveland suburb of Oakwood Village, Ohio.

1984—Graduates from high school; enrolls briefly at Cuyahoga Community College; wins Miss Teen All-America beauty contest.

1986—Wins Miss Ohio beauty contest; earns second place in Miss USA beauty contest; embarks on seven-nation goodwill tour with comedian Bob Hope.

1987—Wins third place in Miss World beauty contest; moves to Chicago to begin a modeling career.

1989—Meets Vincent Cirrincione, who becomes her manager; moves to New York City; gets part in the short-lived television series *Living Dolls*; diagnosed with diabetes.

1991—First major movie role, in *Jungle Fever*.

1991 –1992—Regular part in television series *Knots Landing*.

1993—Marries baseball player David Justice on January 1; stars in television miniseries *Queen*.

1994—Costars in *The Flintstones*.

1995—Costars in *Losing Isaiah*.

1996—Named spokesmodel for Revlon Cosmetics; costars in *Executive Decision*; divorced from David Justice.

1998—Stars in television miniseries *The Wedding*; costars in movie *Bulworth*.

1999—Stars in made-for-television movie *Introducing Dorothy Dandridge*.

2000—Wins Golden Globe and Emmy awards for her performance as Dorothy Dandridge; costars in movie *X-Men*.

2001—Marries singer Eric Benet on January 24; costars in *Swordfish* and *Monster's Ball*.

2002—Wins Academy Award for her role in *Monster's Ball*; costars in James Bond movie *Die Another Day*.

2003—Costars in *X-Men 2*.

2004—Stars in *Catwoman*; divorced from Eric Benet.

2005—Stars in television movie *Their Eyes Were Watching God*; does voice-over for movie *Robots*.

2006—Costars in *X-Men 3*.

Filmography

MOVIES

Jungle Fever, 1991

Strictly Business, 1991

The Last Boy Scout, 1991

Boomerang, 1992

CB4, 1993

Father Hood, 1993

The Program, 1993

The Flintstones, 1994

Losing Isaiah, 1995

Executive Decision, 1996

Race the Sun, 1996

Girl 6, 1996

The Rich Man's Wife, 1996

B*A*P*S, 1997

*Bulworth,*1998

Why Do Fools Fall in Love, 1998

X-Men, 2000

Swordfish, 2001

Monster's Ball, 2001

Die Another Day, 2002

X-Men 2, 2003

Gothika, 2003

Catwoman, 2004

Robots, 2005 (voice-over)

X-Men 3, 2006

TELEVISION

Living Dolls, 1989

Knots Landing, 1991–1992

Queen, 1993

Solomon and Sheba, 1995

The Wedding, 1998

*Introducing Dorothy
    Dandridge*, 1999

*Their Eyes Were Watching
    God*, 2005

Chapter Notes

Author's Note: Most of the magazine articles were accessed through the database EBSCO host.

Chapter 1. "And the Oscar Goes to . . ."

1. Frank Sanello, *Halle Berry: A Stormy Life* (London: Virgin Books, Ltd., 2003), p. 166.

2. Christopher John Farley, *Introducing Halle Berry* (New York: Pocket Books, 2002), p. 199.

3. Ronald Grover, "Why the Oscar Belongs to Halle," *Business Week Online*, March 22, 2002; accessed through EBSCOhost (May 26, 2004).

4. David Hutchings, "Oh, What a Night!" *People*, April 7, 2003, p. 110.

5. Farley, p. 222.

6. Ibid.

Chapter 2. "Beautiful in My Own Right"

1. Frank Sanello, *Halle Berry: A Stormy Life* (London: Virgin Books, Ltd., 2003), p. 5 ; Christopher John Farley, *Introducing Halle Berry* (New York: Pocket Books, 2002), pp. 17–18.

2. Sanello, p. 5.

3. Frank Sanello, "Halle's Secret Pain," *London Mirror*, June 14, 2003, <http://www.mirror.co.uk/news/allnews/page.cfm?objectid=13068518&method=full&siteid=50143> (September 27, 2004).

4. David A. Keeps, "Halle Berry Dishes the Dirt," *Marie Claire*, February 2002.

5. Jim Calio, "Halle's Moment, *Good Housekeeping*, August 2002.

6. Martha Southgate, "Halle Berry Bounces Back," *McCall's*, October 2000, p. 20.

7. "Halle Berry: Her Secret Source of Strength," *Redbook*, March 2003

8. Lawrence Grobel, "Halle Berry," *Playboy*, January 2003, p. 68.

9. Sanello, "Halle's Secret Pain."

10. David Ritz, "Heart to Heart," *Essence*, December 2002, p. 132.

11. Jill Gerston, "The Prom's Co-Queen Finally Gets Her Revenge," *New York Times*, March 12, 1995, p. H27.

12. Ibid.

13. Laura B. Randolph, "Halle Berry," *Ebony*, April 1993, p. 119.

14. Diane Clehane, "Halle's Comet," *Biography*, January 2001, p. 62.

15. Christopher John Farley, *Introducing Halle Berry* (New York: Pocket Books, 2002), p. 32.

16. Author interview with Carl Dunn, CEO, *Pageantry Magazine*, April 14, 2005.

17. Ibid.

18. Malissa Thompson, "Halle's Comet," *McCall's*, March 1996, p. 51.

19. Halle Berry, quoted at <http://www.filmpeople/188683/main?htv=12> (August 25, 2005).

20. Gerston.

21. Grobel,

Chapter 3. Life as a "Human Coat Hanger"

1. Karen S. Schneider, Johnny Dodd, "Hurts So Bad," *People*, May 13, 1996, p. 105.

2. Ibid.

3. "Beauty and the Brave," *Redbook*, July 1994.

4. Ibid.

5. Lawrence Grobel, "Halle Berry," *Playboy*, January 2003, p. 68.

6. Suzanne Ely, "Halle Berry: Her Secret Source of Strength," *Redbook*, March 2003.

7. Jim Calio, "Halle's Moment," *Good Housekeeping*, August 2002.

Chapter 4. And Justice for Halle

1. Bebe Moore Campbell, "Halle Berry: The Inside Story," *Essence*, October 1996, p. 140.

2. Ibid.

3. Christopher John Farley, *Introducing Halle Berry* (New York: Pocket Books, 2002), p. 63.

4. Author interview with Joseph C. Phillips, April 21, 2005.

5. Ibid.

6. Ibid.

7. Ibid.

8. Ibid.

9. Farley, p. 77.

10. Tim Brooks and Earle Marsh, *The Complete Directory to Prime Time Network and Cable TV Shows* (New York: Ballantine Books, 1999), p. 870.

11. Tim Allis, David Hutchings, Andrew Abrahams, "The Woman Who Would Be Queen," *People*, February 22, 1993, p. 35.

12. Kelly Kenyatta, *Red Hot Halle* (Chicago: William H. Kelly Publishing Company, 2003), p. 69.

13. Frank Sanello, *Halle Berry: A Stormy Life* (London: Virgin Books, Ltd., 2003), p. 50.

14. Vincent Coppola, "Beauty and The Brave," *Redbook*, July 1994, p. 48.

15. Ibid.

16. Laura B. Randolph, "Halle Berry," *Ebony*, April 1993.

17. Coppola, p. 50.

Chapter 5. Of Cavemen and Kings

1. Vincent Coppola, "Beauty and the Brave," *Redbook*, July 1994, p. 50.

CHAPTER NOTES

2. Tim Allis, David Hutchings, Andrew Abrahams, "The Woman Who Would Be Queen," *People*, February 22, 1993, p. 35.

3. Richard Zoglin, "Florid Fiction, Bruising Fact," *Time*, February 15, 1993, p. 60.

4. Frank Sanello, *Halle Berry: A Stormy Life* (London: Virgin Books, Ltd., 2003), p. 60.

5. Frank Sanello, "Halle's Secret Pain," *London Mirror*, June 14, 2003, <http://www.mirror.co.uk/news/allnews/page.cfm?objectid=13068518&method=full&siteid=50143> (September 27, 2004).

6. Gilles Bensimon, "The 9 Lives of Halle Berry," *Elle*, October 2003, p. 264.

7. Laura B. Randolph, "Halle Berry," *Ebony*, December 1994.

8. Ibid.

9. Coppola.

10. Randolph.

11. Karen S. Schneider, Johnny Dodd, "Hurts So Bad," *People*, May 13, 1996, p. 108.

12. Lisa Jones, "The Blacker the Berry," *Essence*, June 1994.

13. Jill Gerston, "The Prom's Co-Queen Finally Gets Her Revenge," *New York Times*, March 12, 1995, p. H27.

14. Malissa Thompson, "Halle's Comet," *McCall's*, March 1996, p. 51.

15. Sanello, *Halle Berry: A Stormy Life*, p. 72.

16. Randolph.

17. Ibid.

18. Gerston.

Chapter 6. In the Public Eye

1. Lisa Schwarzbaum, "A Little Too Black and White," *Entertainment Weekly*, March 24, 1995, p. 45.

2. Diane Clehane, "Halle's Comet," *Biography*, January 2001, p. 64.

3. "Halle Berry Stars in Murder Mystery 'The Rich Man's Wife,'" *Jet*, September 2, 1996.

4. Laura B. Randolph, "Halle Berry," *Ebony*, March 1997, p. 24.

5. Bebe Moore Campbell, "Halle Berry: The Inside Story," *Essence*, October 1996, p. 72.

6. Randolph, p. 26.

7. "Encore Presentation: Interviews with Halle Berry, Pierce Brosnan," *CNN Larry King Weekend*, November 16, 2002, <http://www.cnn.com/TRANSCRIPTS/0211/16/lklw.00.html> (June 8, 2004).

8. Randolph, p. 26.

9. Ibid.

10. Merle Ginsberg, "Halle From the Heart," *Ladies' Home Journal*, November 2003, p. 141.

11. "Halle Berry Must Choose Between a Black Man and White Man in TV Movie 'The Wedding,'" *Jet*, February 16, 1998.

Chapter 7. From Star to Superstar

1. Laura B. Randolph, "Halle Berry," *Ebony*, August 1999, p. 90.

2. Annamarie Iverson, "Halle Is Forever," *Harper's Bazaar*, July 1999, p. 110.

3. Randolph, pp. 93–94.

4. "Halle Berry Talks About Portraying Actress Dorothy Dandridge in August Issue of Ebony," *Jet*, July 26, 1999, p. 40.

5. Michael Ventre, "Berry Looks to Expand on Dandridge's Career," *Daily Variety*, February 11, 2000.

6. Christopher John Farley, *Introducing Halle Berry* (New York: Pocket Books, 2002), p. 170.

7. Miki Turner, "10 Burning Questions: Halle Berry," ESPN website, March 24, 2004, <http://sports.espn.go.com/espn/page3/story?page=10bqs/Berry> (April 5, 2005).

8. Kelly Kenyatta, *Red Hot Halle* (Chicago: William H. Kelly Publishing Co., 2003), p. 101.

9. Leslie Marshall, "Halle's Journey," *InStyle*, July 2000.

10. Ibid.

11. "Film Star Berry Escapes Jail," BBC news website, May 11, 2000, <http://news.bbc.co.uk/1/hi/entertainment/744632.stm> (May 18, 2004).

12. Ibid.

13. Farley, p. 184.

14. Laura Randolph, "Halle Berry: On Her Public Troubles, Private Joys and Sudden Desire for a Baby," *Ebony*, August 2000.

15. Gilles Bensimon, "The 9 Lives of Halle Berry," *Elle*, October 2003, p. 258.

16. Tom Brook, "Berry Becomes Bond Golden Girl," BBC news website, November 18, 2002, <http://news.bbc.co.uk/1/hi/entertainment/film/2485595.stm> (May 18, 2004).

17. Kelly Carter, "Berry Isn't Bonded to Any Role," *USA Today*, November 20, 2002.

18. "And the Winner Is . . . ," *London Telegraph*, December 31, 2001, <http://www.opinion.telegraph.co.uk/arts> (November 26, 2004).

19. Sebastian Gutierrez, "Gothika," *Entertainment Weekly*, August 22–29, 2003.

20. "Actress Berry Files for Divorce," BBC News website, April 27, 2004, <http://news.bbc.co.uk/2/hi/entertainment/3663085.stm> (May 27, 2005).

21. "Halle Berry and Benjamin Bratt," *The Oprah Winfrey Show* <http://www.oprah.com> (May 27, 2005).

22. Claudia Puig, "'Catwoman': Like Claws on a Chalkboard," *USA Today*, July 23, 2004, p. 5E.

23. William Keck, "Berry's Career Purrs Along Nicely," *USA Today*, March 4, 2005, p. 3E.

24. Author interview with Jo Laverde, Nielsen Media Research, April 11, 2005.

25. Roger Ebert, "Robots," *Chicago Sun-Time*s, March 11, 2005, <http://rogerebert.suntimes.com> (March 30, 2005).

26. Baker, Rosalie F., "Halle Berry's Dream," *Footsteps*, March/April 2005, vol. 7.

27. Merle Ginsberg, "Halle From the Heart," *Ladies' Home Journal*, November 2003, p. 136.

Further Reading

Carter, Alden. *I'm Tougher Than Diabetes*. Morton Grove, Ill.: Albert Whitman & Company, 2001.

Gaskins, Pearl Fuyo. *What Are You?: Voices of Mixed-Race Young People*. New York: Henry Holt and Company, 1999.

Gogerly, Liz. *Halle Berry*. Oxford, England: Raintree Publishers, 2005.

Naden, Corinne, and Rose Blue. *Halle Berry*. Broomall, Pa.: Chelsea House Publishers, 2001.

Parish, James Robert. *Halle Berry: Actor*. New York: Ferguson Publishing Co., 2004.

Internet Addresses

Halle Berry's official website
<http://www.hallewood.com>

The Internet Movie Database: Halle Berry page
<http://www.imdb.com/name/nm0000932>

Index

INDEX